This journal belongs to:

_____

It's a beautiful day in your neighborhood for meeting new friends, sharing kind thoughts, and being the most caring neighbor you can be. Sometimes you just need a little inspiration to get you started!

With the help of Mister Rogers, your television friend, these pages will guide you to appreciating the good things in yourself, in others, and in the world around you. You don't have to start at the beginning and you don't have to go in order. Just grab your favorite pencil and some crayons, pick a page that appeals to you, and start discovering the neighborhood you call home. Remember to bring along your guardian when venturing outside so you'll stay safe. As Mister Rogers once said, "The more you grow into a helpful person yourself, the happier you'll find this world of ours is." By being the special person you are, you're already making your neighborhood a better place for everyone.

Do you have an after-school routine? Draw it in pictures.

1. _____

_____

_____

"There's so much to wonder about in this world, isn't there?"

_____

_____

What three things do you wonder about? List them here.

2. _____

_____

_____

_____

3. _____

_____

_____

_____

_____

Do you have any favorite make-believe games? Pick one. How would you teach it to someone else?

Choose an item in your kitchen—a drink or food—and think about where it came from. Was it grown or made locally, or did it come from somewhere else? How did it get to your neighborhood? Draw its journey to your kitchen. (If it is milk, for example, you can begin with a picture of a cow.)

Draw a little sketch of
your street. Put in the
places that are most
important to you.

Is there a house you
like to look at? A
neighbor you like to
greet? A good hiding
spot for Hide 'n' Seek?

Bring cookies to the closest firehouse with your family. Write a little thank-you note to go with the package. If the firefighters aren't busy, see if you can introduce yourself and take a picture with them.

PASTE A COPY OF THE PHOTOGRAPH, OR DRAW A PICTURE OF IT FROM MEMORY.

Do you have a favorite tree in the neighborhood? What do you like to do under the tree? Describe those activities here.

What does it mean to be a caring neighbor?

If there is a factory near where you live, what do they make there? Maybe there's a building that used to be a factory but has been converted (changed) into something else. See if you can find out a little about its history. When was it built? What did it produce? When did it change?

Draw a picture of your house or building.

What is the name of your town? When did you move here?

Let's find out
more about your
favorite teachers.
What inspired
them to become
a teacher?

Ask a veteran if you can interview them about their life story. Prepare your list of questions here.

Ask a family member, friend, or neighbor for his or her favorite dessert recipe. Write it down on these recipe cards.

Find out some of the places your parents or other relatives have traveled to. What kind of interesting adventures did they have?

Is there a place you can go nearby to see your neighborhood in a different way? Maybe you can walk to the top of a hill, or take an elevator up to see the view from a tall building. What did you notice from this new perspective?

"If you had all the toys in the world and you didn't have any imagination about how you would play with them, those toys would just sit there doing nothing. And that would be no fun. Thinking up good things to do with what you have gives everybody a good feeling."

Describe your favorite toy.

Do you send letters to other people? Collect some stamps you like from letters that arrive at your house and paste them here.

Do you know
who delivers your
mail? What would
you like to find out
about this person?
Write your questions
here and see if your
mail carrier will
answer them.

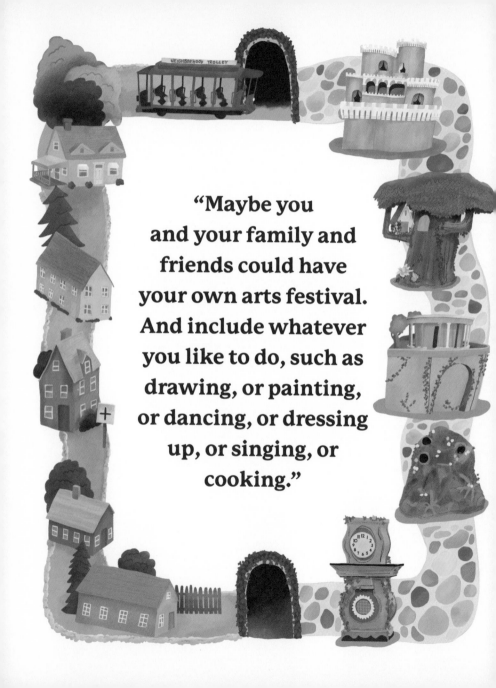

"Maybe you and your family and friends could have your own arts festival. And include whatever you like to do, such as drawing, or painting, or dancing, or dressing up, or singing, or cooking."

Plan out your
arts festival here.
What talents will
it showcase? Who
will participate?

What would you name your own Neighborhood of Make-Believe? What fun things would be in it? What neighbors would live there— real or pretend?

How do you feel when you are hurrying to leave your house, and how do you feel when you are taking your time? Which feels better? If you want to be in less of a hurry, write down some ideas here.

"Every once in a while, do you just like to take your time with what you're doing?"

Look around your neighborhood for artwork. It might be paintings hanging in a café or a sculpture in the middle of a park. Draw something here based on what you found.

What's your favorite song? Capture a few details about it here:

SONG TITLE:

ARTIST:

INSTRUMENTS I CAN HEAR PLAYING:

SONG LYRICS I WANT TO REMEMBER:

> *"**Thank you.**
> Two of the best
> words we can
> ever learn. In fact,
> 'thank you' is
> a way of saying
> 'I love you.'"*

Use the space on the next page to write a thank-you note to someone who recently gave you something or did something special for you. If you'd like, cut out the letter and give it to them.

DEAR _____ ,

_____

_____

_____

_____

_____

_____

_____

_____

_____

_____

_____

YOUR NEIGHBOR,

_____

_____

_____

How do people get around your town— by car, by trolley, by train, or some other way? How are all of those modes of transportation important to your neighbors?

"Real strength has to do with helping others."

What are some of the ways you can help your neighbors? Maybe you and your family members can volunteer at a soup kitchen or collect cans for donation. Brainstorm ideas and pick one to try.

Learn a new game from a family member, friend, or neighbor. It can be a card game, a ball game, a game of jumping rope, or any other kind. Write the instructions here and draw a picture to accompany them.

Write a story with a beginning, a middle, and an ending.

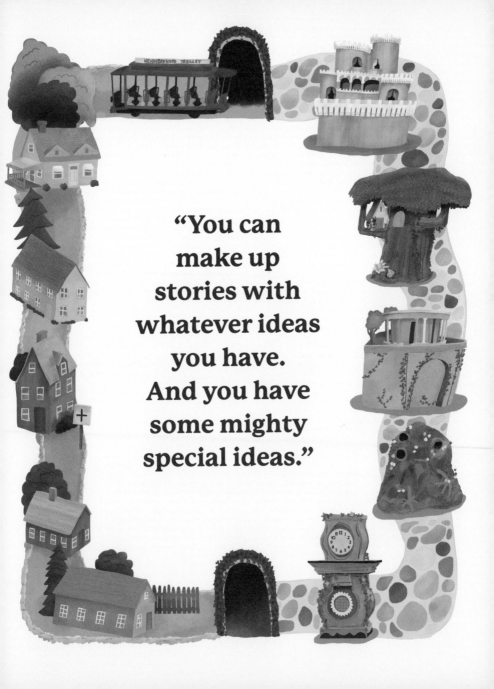

"You can make up stories with whatever ideas you have. And you have some mighty special ideas."

What birthdays are you looking forward to this year (whether it's your own or someone else's)? Write down the dates and other details.

_____

_____

_____

_____

_____

_____

"Birthday presents and birthday parties are really little expressions of love. And it's feeling love that makes somebody feel good. That's the real present."

Who takes care of you during the day and at night?

"It's fun to think about things like birds in the air, fish in the water, and animals and people walking on the earth. Yet all of us are alive, and we all need some kind of care."

With the help of a guardian, pick a day to clean up your neighborhood. See if you can get others to join you. Take a trash bag, some gloves, and maybe some doughnuts to make it more fun. Draw a picture before and after the cleanup so you can remember how much you accomplished together.

BEFORE

Add details about the experience here.

AFTER

"There are many things we can do when we're feeling angry or sad or happy—like exercises, or deep breathing, or music, or sports, or crafts. In fact, they're some of the best things we can ever learn to do."

What kinds of things do you do to express your feelings when you are happy and when you are sad?

Do you have a favorite restaurant in your town?

WHAT IS ITS NAME?

WHEN DID IT OPEN?

DO YOU KNOW THE NAME OF ANYONE WHO WORKS THERE?

WHAT DO YOU LIKE TO ORDER?

WHAT WORK IS DONE TO PREPARE THIS FOOD FOR YOU?

Make a salad with locally grown produce.
Write the recipe here.

How was it?

Plan a neighborhood potluck. Who will your family invite? When would you like it to happen? What would you like folks to bring? Design your invitation below.

What new skill do you want to learn, whether it's learning to play a new instrument, joining a sports team, or speaking a new language? Write down why you want to pursue this activity.

"If there's something you really want to do . . . it's worth all the practice time."

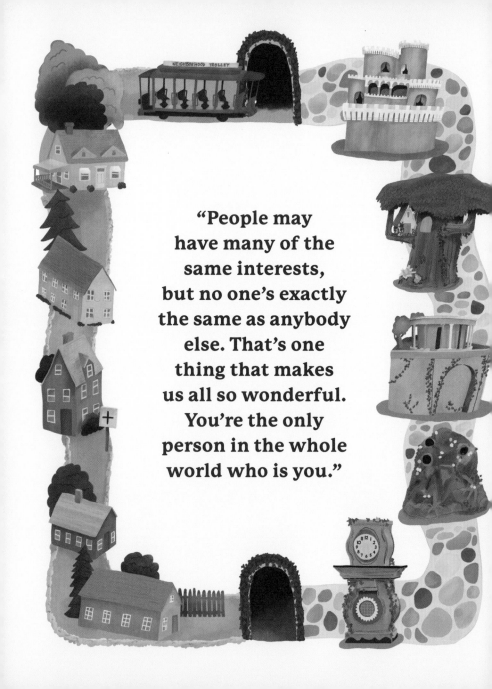

"People may have many of the same interests, but no one's exactly the same as anybody else. That's one thing that makes us all so wonderful. You're the only person in the whole world who is you."

What makes you special and different from everyone else?

Do you have a neighbor
who might need a hand
with some yard work?
With the permission
and guidance of your
guardian, see if the
neighbor would like
some help. Write about
your experience here.

On a weekend, attend a local game of sports, like soccer or basketball, with your family. It doesn't matter if the players are kids or grownups, if it's competitive or just for fun, or if you even know the names of the teams. Just watch for the fun of it. Write about your experience here.

Do you like to take a walk with a specific goal, or just wander around? Decide on a path for a short walk near your house and draw it here. Try it out with your guardian.

You can learn about yourself and the world at the same time by noticing what you like to do when you go for a walk. Write about what you observe while walking outside, such as certain birds, footprints in the snow, favorite trees or shops, or even people you know.

Create another use for something you'd otherwise throw away. What is its new purpose?

"Did you ever try your shoes on your hands? It's fun to think of different things like that, isn't it? It's like playing with ideas. In fact, that's how people invent new things. They just start to play with ideas and let their imaginations have a good time."

Help your family make a shopping list for the store and write it down here. Do you need…

...LAUNDRY DETERGENT?

...TOOTHPASTE?

... SHAMPOO?

- [ ]
- [ ]
- [ ]
- [ ]
- [ ]
- [ ]
- [ ]
- [ ]
- [ ]
- [ ]
- [ ]
- [ ]

- ☐ _____
- ☐ _____
- ☐ _____
- ☐ _____
- ☐ _____
- ☐ _____
- ☐ _____
- ☐ _____
- ☐ _____

Go to the store together.

DO YOU KNOW HOW TO FIND THE ITEM YOU ARE LOOKING FOR?

_____

DID YOU SEE ANYONE STOCKING SHELVES?

_____

MAKE SURE TO CHECK OFF EVERYTHING ON YOUR LIST THAT YOU PURCHASE!

Draw a picture of
yourself greeting
your family after
a long day apart.

How do you feel when you say goodbye to your family? How do you feel when you see them again? Do you like to tell each other what you did in the meantime?

Draw a map of your town, including a new destination for sightseers. What should they look for when they pass this "hidden gem"?

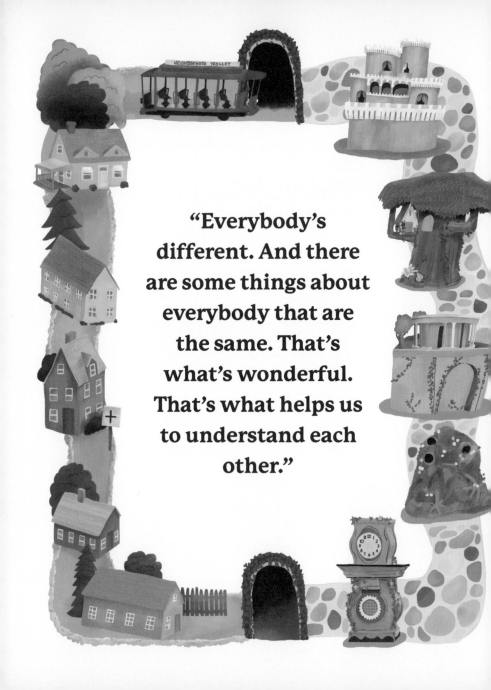

"Everybody's different. And there are some things about everybody that are the same. That's what's wonderful. That's what helps us to understand each other."

Is there someone in your neighborhood who seems very different from you? Write a list of things you have in common with this person.

1.

2.

3.

4.

5.

6.

7.

"Do you like to look at something like a plant really carefully? If you do, that's one way to know you're growing."

Be silent for twenty-five seconds while you look closely at an object you find outside, such as a plant. What details do you notice? Write your observations here.

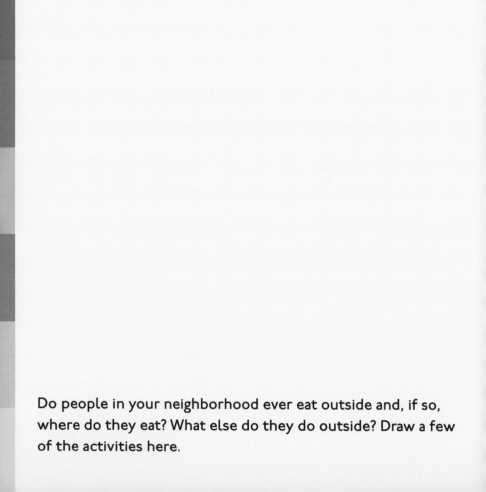

Do people in your neighborhood ever eat outside and, if so, where do they eat? What else do they do outside? Draw a few of the activities here.

Find a patch of grass or empty lot that most people ignore. Take the time to look at it. Brainstorm a list of five possible names for it.

1.

2.

3.

4.

5.

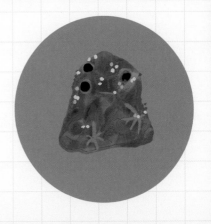

Take a walk and notice
some of the nicest things
about your neighborhood.
Write them down here.

What is special about
each member of your
family? Write the names
of every family member
and list what is special
about each of you.

Is there an item in your house that's broken, whether a shoe or a vacuum? Instead of buying a replacement, see if there's a repair shop in your area and find out what you can about the repair process.

Draw a picture to
show what is broken
and how you think it
might be fixed.

What are some of the things you like about your neighbors?

Look for an example of people around you who are very focused on what they are doing.

WHAT HELPS YOU FOCUS ON ONE THING?

WHAT KINDS OF THINGS MAKE IT DIFFICULT FOR YOU TO FOCUS ON ONE THING?

What kinds of trees grow in your area? Do they lose their leaves? Draw some of the trees here and label them. Draw a close-up of their leaves or needles.

What kinds of birds live in your area? Go outside with your guardian a few minutes earlier than you usually do in the morning and listen to the bird calls.

Can you see the birds? Try drawing the ones you see and labeling them if you can.

If there were a
magic garden near
you, what would
grow there?

Look around today for examples of people helping other people. List as many as you can here. Include everything you see, even something as small as a person picking up a hat that flew off a stranger's head.

1.

2.

3.

4.

5.

6.

7.

"There are
many helpful
people in this world,
aren't there?
The more you grow
into a helpful
person yourself,
the happier you'll
find this world
of ours is."

While you're out with your guardian, take time to say "Thank you" to the helpers in your neighborhood, whether a crossing guard or a baker. Write about how the person reacted and how you felt afterward.

"Haven't you found that the best way to be happy is to be helping somebody else?"

Write down one way you can help someone today. Who will you help and what will you do?

Is there an animal
shelter in your area
that you can visit? Find
out if your family can
volunteer, or donate
some old towels when
you visit. What was
your experience like?

Find out where in your town you can recycle rechargeable batteries, electronics, and other items that can't go in the regular trash or recycling. Design a poster to help spread the word.

PERHAPS YOUR FAMILY COULD HELP YOU COPY THE POSTER
AND HANG IT IN THE LIBRARY OR ON A COMMUNITY BULLETIN BOARD.

With the help of your guardian, reach out to adults who practice make-believe in their professions: writers, actors, or artists. Ask them questions about how they stay creative. Write down their advice.

"Some of
the things that you
feel like doing to
express yourself
when you're little,
you keep developing
all during your
lifetime. That's
one of the great
things about people
growing."

"Isn't it nice when somebody helps you feel good about who you are? If you look for it, you'll probably find something fine inside of everybody."

Who makes you feel good about yourself?

What do you know about the history of your town or city? Who first lived there? Was it a farming community? Did it have an industry? How did it get its name? Capture some of those details here.

With the help of your guardian, interview a neighbor about their childhood.

WHERE DID THEY GROW UP?

_____

_____

_____

WHEN DID THEY MOVE INTO YOUR NEIGHBORHOOD?

_____

_____

_____

WHAT DO THEY MISS ABOUT THEIR CHILDHOOD HOME?

_____

_____

_____

_____

_____

"What kinds of things are you good at helping with? I remember one child telling me one day, 'Mister Rogers, I'm only four years old, but I can do some kind things.' She was learning to be a helper. And I trust that you are, too."

Are there ways you can help your neighbors or your family now? What about when you are a grown-up?

What is one new thing you learned today? How did it make you feel?

"Somehow learning seems to make you feel good about yourself."

Do you have a pet? Draw a picture of it here. What do you do to take care of it? If you don't have a pet, make an imaginary one and draw it here. What will its name be?

Neighbor Aber once said, "When anybody's in trouble, we try to do what we can." Go through your clothes, books, and toys and set aside items you no longer use or need. Where in your community can you and your family bring these donations to help someone else? If you can donate, write about how it feels to know someone else will love these items.

Is there a nursing home or senior center that accepts visitors? Plan a visit with your family. Pick one of the activities below to do there and write about your experience.

- PERFORM A SONG
- PERFORM A DANCE
- PERFORM A MARTIAL ARTS ROUTINE
- BRING ARTWORK
- BRING COOKIES
- HAVE A CONVERSATION

_____

_____

_____

_____

_____

_____

_____

_____

_____

_____

_____

_____

While you are there, ask if you can spend some time getting to know one or two of the residents. Write down a few questions that you'd like to ask someone who was born before most homes had televisions. Chances are you'll hear some incredible stories.

"Passing things at the table or getting your mom's pocketbook or briefcase when she asks for it—or giving someone a hug when you think they need one. That's being a caregiver. You see, you're already a caregiver, by many things that you do."

List one thing you can do to help take care of your family, friends, school, and neighborhood:

FAMILY:

FRIENDS:

SCHOOL:

NEIGHBORHOOD:

Find someone who celebrates a different holiday from you. Find out what you can about that holiday. What are some of the traditions? Foods? Important characters? Write about it here.

What languages other than English do people speak in your area? Find someone who speaks a language you don't know.

WHAT IS IT?

WHERE IS IT SPOKEN?

ASK IF HE OR SHE COULD TEACH YOU A FEW WORDS.

WRITE THE NEW WORDS HERE SO YOU WILL REMEMBER THEM.

Is there a working farm near you that you could visit?
What do they grow or produce there? Draw a picture.

If there aren't farms, are there any farmer's markets you can visit?

WHAT IS SOLD THERE?

WHAT WOULD YOU LIKE TO SELL IF YOU HAD A SPOT AT THIS MARKET?

What is something you care passionately about? Make up some slogans to help others recognize the urgency of the issue.

Now draw a poster that supports your cause.

Do you and your family help out neighbors when they are away perhaps by feeding their cats or watering their plants? Would you like to?

What kinds of
favors do your
neighbors do
for you?

When a new neighbor moves in, it's nice to bring a treat over. What are some treats you and your family could make the next time someone new moves in? List them here.

Who works at nighttime in your neighborhood? Doctors and firefighters? Who else might just be getting dressed to head to work as you're brushing your teeth to get ready for bed? What do you think it would be like to work at night and sleep during the day?

Do your elders remember any make-believe games they used to play? What were they?

We have roots in the places where we live. What do trees' roots do? What would happen if a tree didn't have strong roots? What are some ways you can strengthen your own roots in your neighborhood?

Write down three ways you're important:

1.

2.

3.

"If you could only sense how important you are to the lives of those you meet— how important you can be to the people you may never even dream of."

If a guest visits your house, what is the first thing you'd like to show them? What can you tell them about it?

> "Isn't it wonderful the things that people can make?"

What kinds of things can you make?

What do you like to do when friends stop by your home?

Do you have enough time each day to talk with your family? How can you make more time for conversation?

> "Nobody can have everything. That's why it's important for us to learn to make good choices."

What good choices did you make today?

What kinds of activities do people in your neighborhood like to do in the summer? What about in the winter?

What do you like to share with other people?

Think about the things you like to share and those you don't. What makes them different?

"I like to learn things. Don't you? And there's so much in this world we can learn, no matter how young or how old we are."

What is something you've been trying to learn how to do? How long have you been practicing? What do you think about your progress?

_____

_____

_____

_____

_____

_____

_____

_____

_____

_____

_____

_____

_____

_____

Your guardians are grown up, but that doesn't mean they are done growing. Ask them what they wanted to be when they grew up, then draw a picture to illustrate it.

What are some
of the ways
they still want
to grow?

Do you have friends who live far away? How do you stay in touch with them? What are some other ways to stay in touch?

What are some of
the jobs you see
people doing in your
neighborhood? What
do you think your
neighborhood would
be like if one of these
people stopped doing
their job?

Do you wish you could do something grown-ups do?

"Little or big,
you always
have people who
love you."

Do you think grown-ups wish they could do something you get to do? Draw a picture of a grown-up trying to do something you get to do.

What kinds of books do you like to read? Visit the library with a guardian. What topics interest you? List them here.

Find some books related to your interests; maybe it's whales or outer space. Have some fun browsing, too. You never know what might catch your eye. If you have room at home, make a special space on the shelf for library books. Write about what you've learned from the books you've borrowed.

Next time you are at the playground or lunchroom, look around to see if anyone seems to be alone, looking for company. Invite that person to join you. What is his or her name? What are his or her hobbies? Do you like any of the same games or music? Write a little bit about this new neighbor of yours.

Set a timer for one minute. During that time, try not to say a word. Look at the world around you, and listen to all the sounds. When the minute is up, write down what you saw, what you heard, and how you feel.

"Some of us must have forgotten how nourishing silence can be."

What time does the
sun set tonight? Can
you see the moon?
What are some of the
things you like to do
to get ready for the
night?

"Often when you think you're at the end of something, you're at the beginning of something else."

What might be ending, such as a school year, calendar year, or an extracurricular activity? What new things are beginning?

"I'm interested to know what people do with greeting cards when people get them."

Have you received any greeting cards? How do you feel when you get one?

Do you know how to write in cursive? Ask your parents, relatives, or friends to write a few words in cursive here, then copy the words below theirs. Isn't it elegant?

Does everyone help clean up in your house? What are some of the clean-up jobs? Make a list of the outside jobs here. Add a star next to the ones that can you help with.

Who takes care of the outside of your house? Does someone rake leaves? Clear off snow? What do you think it is like to work outside?

List all the people you see working to keep your neighborhood clean. Some might be sweeping the sidewalks. Someone might be picking up the trash. Others might be washing windows.

WHAT WOULD YOUR NEIGHBORHOOD BE LIKE WITHOUT THESE WORKERS?

HOW CAN YOU EXPRESS YOUR GRATITUDE FOR THE WORK THEY DO?

Collect some boxes and other materials. Instead of recycling them right away, think of what you could make. How about a town? A robot? A dollhouse? Draw a sketch above of something you could make and then try it out.

Does your town have a community center or does your building have a community room? Visit and see what activities they offer. List some of them here.

Are there any activities you would like to try? Which ones?

Are there any historical monuments or plaques in your town? Take an afternoon to visit them with your family and read about what might have happened there. Try taking a rubbing of some of the engraved words on the plaque if you are allowed and paste it into your journal here.

Write a bit about what you learned.

Put on a show! Ask everyone to come with something to perform. There are no judges, only performers. Everyone can do something, whether it's making a silly sound, telling a joke, or playing the violin.

Pick something in your house that you've never looked at carefully. Maybe it's a piece of art on the wall or a coffee table book full of photographs. Maybe it's a souvenir from another country. Examine it closely and draw a picture of it here.

Does your family have a garden or access to a community garden? What do you grow? If you don't have a garden, what ideas have you grown in your mind?

_____

_____

_____

_____

_____

_____

_____

_____

_____

_____

_____

_____

_____

_____

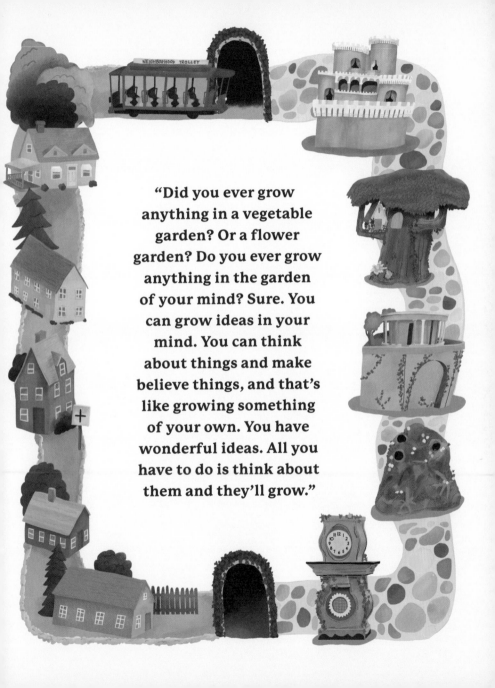

"Did you ever grow anything in a vegetable garden? Or a flower garden? Do you ever grow anything in the garden of your mind? Sure. You can grow ideas in your mind. You can think about things and make believe things, and that's like growing something of your own. You have wonderful ideas. All you have to do is think about them and they'll grow."

Are the streets near your home named for people, places, or things? Draw some of the street signs here.

Find out more about a street in your neighborhood named for a person. Who was this person and what did they do?

Where are the public spaces in your town? Are there parks, playgrounds, schools, libraries, museums? List some ways you can support these public spaces to keep them nice for everyone to enjoy.

Is there any construction
going on near you? If so,
what is being built and
what kinds of machines
are being operated?
Draw one of them here.

Draw a map showing places a dog might find important in your neighborhood: where to see squirrels, grassy areas, houses where other dogs live.

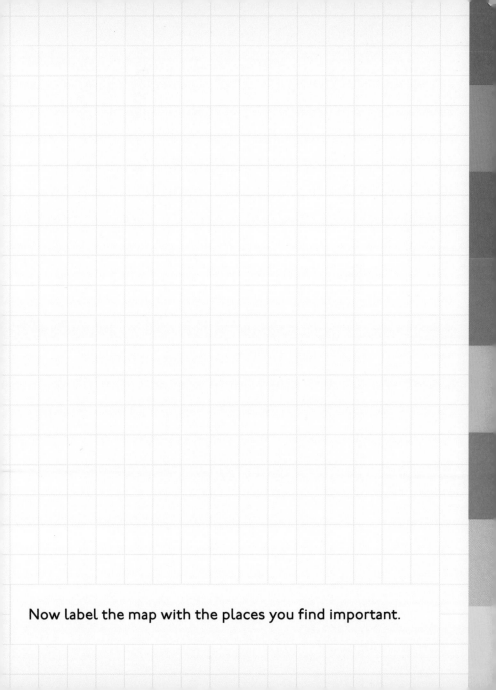

Now label the map with the places you find important.

Do you live in a noisy place or a quiet place or somewhere in between? What sounds do you hear when you walk outside your door?

Listening carefully for a few minutes, write down the sounds you hear outside. Try again at a different time of day. Label both sets of notes with the time.

TIME:

TIME:

What are some of the traditional foods your family makes? Are they served at special occasions? Write down one of the recipes here and include a little story to go with it.

What hobbies do you see people in your neighborhood doing outside in their free time?

Who makes the cakes for your parties? Is there a bakery near your house? With your family, visit a bakery one day, and look at all the pretty things they make. Would you like to decorate cakes in a bakery?

Draw a picture of a decorative cake you'd like to make.

What is your schedule like on a typical weekday? Write it here.

TIME	ACTIVITY

What things do you
like to think about
while you wait?

_____

_____

_____

_____

_____

_____

_____

_____

_____

_____

_____

_____

_____

"Sometimes
it's fun to wait
because you
can think about
things."

"I hope you're proud of yourself for the times you've said yes."

What did you say yes to today?

What makes you feel welcome when you come home?

"It's good
to be curious
about many
things."

List ten things that you are curious about. When you have free time, choose one and explore it.

1.

2.

3.

4.

5.

6.

7.

8.

9.

10.

Who makes dinner in your house? Do you help? If not, would you like to? Why or why not? What are some of your family's favorite meals?

List some of the things you have in your life that you are grateful for.